THE ROAD TO BETHLEHEM

Told by Elizabeth Laird
Foreword by Terry Waite, M.B.E.

AN ETHIOPIAN NATIVITY

Henry Holt and Company   New York

The author and publishers would like to thank all those who
advised on and contributed to the making of this book, especially
the staff of The British Library, David McDowall, Dr. Richard
Pankhurst, and Diana Spencer.

The illustrations in this book are taken from
the following manuscripts, all of which are in The British Library:
OR 602, OR 603, OR 607, OR 646, ADD 24188. The pictures have
been selected for their beauty and suitability and are reproduced
by kind permission of The British Library.

The story is not an exact translation of the text in the
manuscripts from which it has been taken.

Royalties from this book are being donated to Oxfam.

Text copyright © 1987 by Elizabeth Laird
Design copyright © 1987 by William Collins Sons and Co., Ltd.
All rights reserved, including the right to reproduce this
book or portions thereof in any form.
Published in the United States by
Henry Holt and Company, Inc., 521 Fifth Avenue,
New York, New York 10175.

Library of Congress Catalog Card Number: 87-45112
ISBN 0-8050-0539-0

First American Edition

Designer: Enid Fairhead
Printed in Hong Kong by South China Printing Co.
1   3   5   7   9   10   8   6   4   2

Foreword

Ethiopia is a land of stories. Many have been passed from
parents to children across the generations: others have been
recorded in distinctive works of art. In the paintings, as in the
stories, there is a definite Ethiopian element. During visits to
Ethiopia I have collected some of the distinctive painted
panels. They are vivid and colourful. The people of this
unique African country have taken the stories to their hearts.
As they have fashioned them, so they have been fashioned
by them.

Elizabeth Laird has produced a beautiful book, which
brings together the ancient Ethiopian Christian stories and
works of art. As we read, we can trace the Gospel narrative as
recorded in the Bible. We are also enriched by the charming
and tender extras included in these stories. Read with an open
mind, they both delight and inspire. They also remind us that
Ethiopia is a land where long history and culture, out of
centuries of suffering, have produced something of beauty
and dignity.

I hope this book will increase compassion and enlarge
respect for a people who can be justly proud of their traditions.

Terry Waite, M.B.E.

*The Archbishop of Canterbury's Secretary
for Anglican Communion Affairs*

LAMBETH PALACE, DECEMBER 1986

Back in the Middle Ages, when knights in armor jousted with each other, and went off to the Crusades to fight the Saracens, strange stories were told about a fabulous Christian empire somewhere beyond the kingdoms of the Turks. It was ruled, people thought, by a great and powerful king who was called Prester John.

When Portuguese travelers first explored Ethiopia several hundred years later, they thought they had found the land of Prester John. They did not come upon the rich treasures they had been expecting, but they did find a great Christian kingdom, full of churches, monasteries and ancient books, because Ethiopia had been Christian for many, many centuries. It is, in fact, one of the oldest Christian countries in the world.

If you look at a map of Africa, you will find that in the old days there were two possible ways to get to Ethiopia from Europe. One way was to travel up the Nile, and then climb up the rocky plateau on which Ethiopia lies. The other way was to sail down the Red Sea, then strike inland.

Early Christianity reached Ethiopia by both of these two routes. Saints, monks and priests came by sea from Syria, and also along the Nile from Egypt. They brought with them stories about Jesus and his disciples, and the teachings and writings of their own church fathers.

In the very earliest days of Christianity, there were many different records of the life of Jesus and the beginnings of the church. Some of them had been written by the apostles themselves, or by people who had actually witnessed the events they described. These writings were generally agreed to be a true account, and were eventually gathered together to form the New Testament. But other stories and legends were often told as well, and the church discouraged people from reading them.

In Ethiopia, however, which was many months' journey from other Christian lands, there was no such discouragement. People wanted to hear more and more about the life of Jesus, and about his mother, Mary, for whom they felt a deep love and veneration. The Ethiopians based their faith on the New Testament Gospels, as all Christians do, but they also listened eagerly to other stories about Jesus and his mother, some of which you will find in this book.

These stories came from different parts of the ancient world. The description of the Virgin Mary's appearance was written by a bishop of Cyprus who was born in the year 320. The travels of the Holy Family in Egypt were very popular with Egyptians, who built churches and monasteries all along the route which they believed the Holy Family had followed. The story of the two thieves probably came from medieval Europe. The story of the pearl seems to be Ethiopian in origin.

The kings and queens of Ethiopia, who loved these stories as much as the ordinary people, commissioned artists to illustrate them and scribes to write them in large, handsome books. The pictures you see in this book are taken from such handpainted manuscripts, which were made over two hundred years ago.

The Ethiopians who wrote down these stories and painted these pictures loved, as we love, to hear about the angel who came to Mary, the shepherds on the hillside, and the wise men who followed the star, and they worshipped, as we worship, the baby Jesus at Bethlehem.

E.L.

Two of Mary's ancestors are sitting side by side on a low couch with their right hands raised in the traditional gesture of blessing. They each hold a strip of cloth, which shows that they are important people.

✠ ✠ ✠

In the beginning, God made the earth, the heavens and the Garden of Life. And when everything was finished, he made our father Adam, and in his body he placed a white Pearl. The Pearl was passed from generation to generation through the bodies of Noah and Enoch, Abraham, Isaac and Jacob, David and Solomon, until it came to Joachim. And Joachim passed the Pearl to his wife Hannah, and in her body the Pearl grew into a child, and she was the Virgin Mary.

When Mary was still a little girl, her mother Hannah took her to live in the temple in Jerusalem. There, Zachariah the priest and Simeon the holy man taught her to read and pray, and live a holy life.

Mary grew to be full of grace. She was of medium height, with a face the color of ripe wheat. Her eyes were brown and bright, and her eyebrows black and arched. Her face was oval and her nose was long. She spoke clearly and fearlessly, and was seldom angry. She was simple, and humble, she wore plain, homespun clothes, and she listened to people when they talked to her.

Mary as a young girl sits in the temple. The priests are discussing her future. The man standing up has a heart full of jealousy, and that is why he is painted side view. Wicked people are often drawn with only one eye showing in Ethiopian pictures.

One day, when Mary was with two women, a thirsty dog came near them. The two women drove him away, but Mary was sad when she saw how thirsty he was, and she wept.

She fetched her water pot, took off her shoe and poured water into it. Then she gave it to the dog.

"This water," said Mary, "did not come from a well but from heaven, and it was God who gave this thirsty dog water to drink."

"Your heart is much kinder than ours," the women said, "and one day you will be the Mother of Christ, the Messiah."

Chairs like the one on which Mary is sitting were seats of honor for important people, and were considered to be personal possessions. No one else would be allowed to sit in the same chair.

Portraits of two people together
are often shown under a canopy-like
roof in this way. Ethiopian churches
still have decorations on their rooftops
like the one shown in the picture.

When Mary had lived in the temple for twelve years, the time came for her to be married.

The holy man, Joseph the carpenter, was chosen to be her husband, but he went to Zachariah the priest and said, "How can I marry Mary? For I am an old man, and she is a young girl. If I marry her, everyone will laugh at me."

But Zachariah said sternly to Joseph, "You must not question the will of God."

So Joseph and Mary were betrothed, and until the time of her marriage, she went to live in his house. But Joseph went away on a journey.

One day, when Mary went to fetch water at the well, God sent the Angel Gabriel to her.

"Peace be on you," said the Angel, "for God is with you."

Mary turned to the right, and she turned to the left, but she could not see anyone, for no one was there at all. So Mary was frightened, and she dropped her water pot, and ran home to pray.

The Angel came to her again, and his presence filled the courtyard. His wings shone, and his eyes were brighter than the sun.

"Do not be afraid, Mary," he said, "for God is pleased with you. The Holy Spirit will come upon you, and you will have a child. He will be holy, and he will be called the Son of the Most High, and his name will be Jesus, and he will save the people from their sins. He will be the joyful one in whom there is no sorrow. He will be the healthy one, in whom there is no sickness. He will be the blessed one in whom there is no evil, and at his coming, he will light up the whole world."

And Mary said to the Angel, "Why should he come to me? For I am not the daughter of a king."

And the Angel said, "He could have chosen to live with the rich, but he has chosen to be the friend of the poor."

And Mary said, "Here I am, the servant of the Lord, and my soul is in his hands."

In Ethiopian paintings, saints, prophets, kings and angels are often shown being transported on little clouds, as the Archangel is here.

The artist who painted this picture probably copied Mary's prayer stool, and the Archangel's lily, from an earlier Italian painting.

Now Mary was weaving scarlet wool to make curtains for the temple. And when she had finished she took it to Zachariah the priest, and he blessed her. Then Mary went to Elizabeth her cousin, the wife of Zachariah, who was also expecting a child.

When Elizabeth saw Mary, she opened the door to her, and begged her to come in.

"Why has the mother of my Lord come to see me?" she said. "When I heard your voice, I felt my baby leap for joy inside me."

And Mary stayed for three months in the house of her cousin Elizabeth. But when Joseph came back from his journey and found that Mary was expecting a child, he was very angry.

"This is no child of mine," he said.

For a long time, he prayed, and wept, and looked up to heaven, and then he went to sleep. And while he was asleep, the Angel came to him and said, "Do not be angry, Joseph, for Mary's child is of the Holy Spirit, and he shall save people from their sins."

Ethiopian artists did not try to make trees, houses and countryside look realistic. They concentrated on the people, who were the most important part of the picture. Here, the golden sky and red rocks are unreal, but they make a brilliant background to Joseph's curled up figure.

Some months later, Herod the king sent out his officers to bring each person into their own city. So Joseph brought a donkey, and he sat Mary on it, and they started out along the road to Bethlehem.

After they had been traveling for a while, Joseph turned and looked back at Mary, and she was smiling and laughing.

"The baby is about to be born!" she said.

"What shall we do? Where shall we go?" said Joseph.

He looked around, and he saw a cave, where animals were kept, and he led Mary to it.

Then Joseph went off to find a midwife. As he went along the road, the earth trembled, and the oxen and sheep stood looking up to heaven.

When Joseph came back to the cave with the midwife, a great light was shining out of it, and a cloud of light surrounded Mary and the Baby, who was lying in a manger.

And God sent another woman to Mary, her cousin Salome, and she bowed down to the ground. The donkey and the ox bowed their heads to the Child also, and warmed him with their breath.

The artist has painted the Nativity scene in a rocky place, rather than a cave. You can see the cloud of light (over Joseph's head) and the gift of a goat which Salome has brought. Since the picture is 200 years old, it is not surprising that some paint has rubbed off the bottom of Joseph's robe.

The angels are bringing food to Mary in beautifully woven baskets like the ones which Ethiopians still make and use today.

And companies of angels and archangels, the Cherubim and Seraphim, bowed down and worshipped the Child and his mother.

"This is the day that God has made and blessed," they said.

After them came Gabriel, with a bright and shining face. And he bowed down and worshipped.

"It is as I told you," he said. "This is the Child I spoke of when I came to you before. This is the one who will give strength to his people."

And Salome picked the Baby up in her arms and said, "Happy am I to have seen this day, and happy are you, Mary, to be his mother. I will be your servant, and I will never leave you, and I will look after you till I die."

And the angels appeared to herdsmen who were looking after their animals. And when they had heard the news, the herdsmen came and worshipped.

"You are the Savior of the world, the Son of God," they said. "Happy are we to see your glory."

Then all the companies of angels and archangels sang,

"Glory to God in the Heavens, and peace on earth to the children of men, with whom he is pleased."

At night, Ethiopians keep their cattle and sheep in pens, like the one in the picture, to protect them from hyenas and other wild animals, which frequently attack them.

After eight days, the Child was circumcised, according to the Law. And he was named Jesus, as the Angel had said.

And there were three wise men who journeyed from the East. Their names were Tanisuram, Maliko and Zesesba. They traveled from one town and city to another, making inquiries about the Child.

"Where is Christ to be born?" they said, "for we have seen his star in the East and have come to worship him."

When Herod the king heard of this he was angry, and he called the nobles, the priests, the scribes and the elders, and asked them where Christ would be born.

"In Bethlehem," they said, "as the prophets foretold."

Herod said to the wise men, "Go and look for the Child, and when you have found him, come and tell me, so that I may worship him too."

The wise men left Herod, and the star they had followed from their own country guided them to the house where the Child was. And when they saw him in the arms of his Mother, they bowed down and worshipped him, and full of joy, they opened up their treasure bags.

They gave him gold, because he was a king. They gave him frankincense, because he was God. They gave him myrrh because he was a man. And the Child accepted their gifts.

The wise men left the house and began their journey back to Herod. But on their way, while they were sleeping, the Angel of the Lord appeared to them in a dream.

"Do not go back to Herod," he said, "but go straight home to your own country."

And so they did.

The kings have uncovered their heads as a sign of respect. Ethiopians believe that the three kings were descended from Ham, Shem and Japheth, the three sons of Noah, and so they represented all the people in the world.

The buildings in the background look rather like the palaces at Gondar, where the Ethiopian Emperors were living when these pictures were painted.

The king is receiving advice from his courtiers. His crown is in the same style as those which Ethiopian Emperors used to wear. The wicked adviser (painted side view) standing behind the king is carrying a Turkish scimitar. In those days, the Turks and the Ethiopians were enemies.

✤ ✤ ✤

Herod waited two years for the wise men to return, and when they did not he was very angry, and his servants were all afraid. Then Satan spoke to him, and said, "Tomorrow, early in the morning, send your servants to kill every child under two years old in Bethlehem. Then Jesus is sure to die, and he will not grow up to take away your kingdom."

That same night, an Angel appeared to Joseph, and said, "Get up, and take the young Child and his Mother, and go to the land of Egypt, for Herod is looking for the Child and wants to kill him."

So Joseph did as the Angel said, but Herod did as Satan said and killed all the boys of Bethlehem of two years old or less. Only Elizabeth, the wife of Zachariah, escaped with John her son, and Mary, with Jesus her Son.

The Archangel here is Uriel, who guarded the Holy Family on their journey into Egypt. He is holding a cross like the ones Ethiopian priests usually carry.

The road to Egypt was long, and the journey wearisome. Joseph walked in front to show the way, and Mary walked behind with Salome, who had followed them into Egypt.

Sometimes Mary carried the Child on her back, sometimes on her shoulders, and sometimes in her arms, and sometimes Salome carried him in turn.

Mary would set him down on the ground to walk by himself, and he would walk a little way at a time, holding the hem of her skirt. Then he would lift up his arms, as children do who ask their mothers to carry them. And Mary would pick him up and kiss him and carry him again.

Joseph's heart grew tired because of the length of the road. "I am too old," he said. "I cannot go on."

But Mary put the Child into his arms, and Joseph lifted him onto his shoulder, and he forgot that he was tired, and he kissed the Child from his head to his feet, and went on again, with new strength.

This picture shows one of the Holy Family's sufferings on the road. People who had heard of the miracles which Mary had performed thought she was a sorceress, and they were afraid. They put sharp arrows on the road, but Mary took the hand of her Child, and walked through unharmed.

Salome is carrying the bread basket on her head, as Ethiopians still do when they travel.

Now when the Holy Family arrived in Egypt, they sat down under a tree, outside the city, to rest from the heat of the sun, and they slept.

Then the people came out of the city nearby, and some were angry and tried to drive the Holy Family away. But others brought out the sick and those who were possessed by evil spirits, and Mary cured them all of their illness. The dumb spoke, the lame ran, the deaf heard and the blind could see.

Then Mary blessed the rocks, and a spring of water welled up. And Mary said,

"By this water you will be healed, until the end of the world."

And from that time on, sick people came to the spring, and when they drank the water they were healed immediately. Even their animals, their cattle and their horses, were cured of all their illness.

As the Child traveled through Egypt with Mary his Mother, and Joseph and Salome, the mountains and the wild animals came to worship him. And as they journeyed on, the mountains and the wild animals followed him.

So Jesus turned toward them, and he put his hand on the mountain in the east, and his other hand on the mountain in the west, and they stood still, and fixed their roots deep in the rock.

The Ethiopians painted the animals they knew, which included the elephants, monkeys and wild pigs in this picture.

Ethiopians often painted Jesus feeding from his mother's breast, as he is doing here.

One day, as the Holy Family went along a mountain path at sunset, two thieves rushed out upon them with swords drawn. They snatched the Child from the arms of his Mother, and stripped off his clothes. They stole Mary's headcloth, and Salome's too, and as Joseph stood there like a simple sheep they snatched his clothes as well. Then the two thieves went away a short distance, and began plotting together.

Mary was afraid, and she began to cry. One of the thieves saw her weeping, and he said to the other, "Friend and brother, let us not steal their clothes, for this Child is like the son of a king, and I have never seen another like him."

But the other thief said, "No, let us keep the clothes, for they are purple, and fine, and the merchants will pay us well for them."

The first thief said, "We have always robbed together, and last night we took a lot of booty. I will give you my share if you will let me give back the clothes to the Child. I cannot bear to see him standing naked."

So the second thief agreed, and he gave all the clothes back, and Mary joyfully dressed her Son again.

Many years later, the two thieves were crucified with Jesus, one on the right, and the other on the left, and the thief who had shown mercy to the Child entered straight into the Garden of Paradise.

The lines across the picture are showing through from the other side
of the vellum page. The scribe who wrote the story in this
manuscript scratched lines on the page before he started work to
keep his writing straight.

Herod discovered that Joseph and Mary and the Child Jesus
were hiding from him in the desert, and he was glad that at
last he knew where they were. He called his nobles and said to
them, "Get up at dawn, and we will surround the desert."

But the Angel of God came to Joseph in a dream and warned
him to flee to Mt. Lebanon with the Child and his Mother.

Herod ordered his soldiers to surround Mt. Lebanon, and
they hunted for the Holy Family, but they could not find them
among the rocks, the dense forests or the holes in the ground.

"What has become of them?" said Herod. "Has the earth
swallowed them up?"

Then Herod sent a herald around the city to cry out, "If anyone finds these people, and brings them to me, I will give him half of my kingdom."

The soldiers scattered themselves in the hills and valleys, but they did not find them. So Herod returned to the city. But the Angel of God stood in the road, and struck the horse's nose with a piece of wood, and the horse leaped up into the air, and threw Herod onto the ground. The soldiers put Herod on a bed, and took him back to his house, but although he was sick, it was not yet time for him to die.

Ethiopian artists sometimes showed several events at once. This picture starts on the right, and shows the Archangel hitting the horse's nose, and Herod on the ground. On the left hand side, his servants are carrying him away. They are holding over him the ceremonial umbrella of an Ethiopian Emperor.

And when at last Herod died, the Angel Gabriel appeared to
Joseph, and said, "Get up now, and go back to Bethlehem, for
all those who tried to kill the Child are dead."

So Joseph and Mary and the Child, and Salome their cousin,
journeyed back to the land of Israel, to a city named Nazareth.
And there Joseph worked in his carpenter's shop, and the Son
of God worked with him.

✤ ✤ ✤

This book is due on the last date stamped on
the card in the pocket.